THE DEBT-FREE JOURNEY

How Debt Elimination Can Set You Free

MICHAEL SCHULZ

SCHULZ PUBLISHING

CONTENTS

CHAPTER ONE

EPILOGUE

"You can't go back and change the beginning, but you can start where you are and change the ending."

–Clive Staples Lewis

CHAPTER TWO

INTRODUCTION - WINNING THE DEBT BATTLE:

A CHAMPION'S GUIDE TO FINANCIAL FREEDOM

A re you tired of feeling like a prisoner of your debt? Does the weight of unpaid bills keep you up at night? You're not alone. Millions struggle with the burden of debt, feeling trapped and unsure how to break free. I was once, like you are now, full of anxiety and fear of the financial obligations I was committed to.

There were times I felt like there was more month than money, and I wasn't sure how I was going to survive the next day, let alone the next week. Maybe you feel similarly, living paycheck to paycheck, drowning in a sea of debt and bills. But listen up, winner! There's good news: you can take control, rewrite your financial story, and achieve the victory of a debt-free life.

This book is your personal battle plan. We'll equip you with the knowledge and strategies to conquer debt, just like any other challenge you've faced. Our primary goal is to get you into the GOOD—Get Out of Debt—feeling and start living a life free of financial struggles! Remember, winners are prepared. So, let's get started by understanding the enemy: debt itself.

Debt can come in many forms—credit cards, student loans, mortgages—each with its own story. Some debts, like a mortgage for your dream home, can be investments in your future. But others, like credit card debt with sky-high interest, can become chains that hold you back. The key is to recognize the differences and make informed decisions.

Here's the truth, winners: debt doesn't just impact your bank account. It's a mental and emotional battle as well. It steals your peace of mind, strains relationships, and keeps you from reaching your full potential.

The number one cause of marital disagreements surrounds money—more like the lack of money—and where to spend it on paying stuff off. But just like any champion, you can find the motivation to fight back. Understanding how debt affects you is the first step to defeating it.

Now, let's get down to brass tacks. A true winner always assesses the situation. We need to take a good, hard look at your income, expenses, and, yes, even your current debt load.

We know this task may raise unwanted emotions and truths you don't want to face. But this isn't about shame but gathering intelligence for victory. Knowing these numbers empowers you to create a battle plan—a budget that maximizes your resources and prioritizes the debts you'll conquer first.

Remember, champions don't win alone. This book will be your trusted advisor, guiding you through proven strategies like the snowball and avalanche methods. We'll set clear goals because winners need a target.

But conquering debt requires more than just defense. It's about offense, too. We'll explore increasing your income and negotiating better terms with creditors.

There will be setbacks, that's inevitable. Things happen, life occurs, and some plans don't go as expected. But winners are resilient. We'll equip you with the tools to stay motivated and overcome obstacles.

Finally, victory isn't just about eliminating debt. It's about building a secure future. We'll show you how to create an emergency fund to handle unexpected expenses, adopt smart spending habits to ensure you live within your means, how to avoid new debt, and invest in your financial well-being.

This book is your roadmap to financial freedom. By learning about the different types of debt, its impact on your mental and emotional well-being, and the true cost of carrying debt, you'll be better prepared to take control of your financial situation. So, are you ready to win the debt battle and claim your financial victory? Let's turn the page and begin!

CHAPTER THREE

THE DEBT DRAGON:

UNDERSTANDING YOUR ENEMY

W inners know their opponents. In the battle for financial freedom, debt is the dragon you must slay. This chapter equips
you with the knowledge to recognize its forms, understand its tactics,
and grasp the actual cost it exacts.

The Two Faces of Debt: Friend or Foe?

Debt isn't inherently bad. It can be a tool, a temporary boost, to help
you achieve your goals. A mortgage, for instance, can be a stepping
stone to homeownership, building equity over time. Using student
loans wisely can unlock educational opportunities and increase your
earning potential. These are examples of good debt—investments in
your future that yield long-term benefits.

From a business aspect, good debt can be investment debt. A great
example is rental property. Let's say you purchase a single-family home

through a mortgage or home-equity line of credit (HELOC), fix the place, and then rent it out to tenants. If the rent is greater than the total monthly cost of the house—mortgage, interest, insurance, and maintenance fees—then you will have a net positive cash flow into your bank account. Using the renter to pay your monthly costs is called Other People's Money (OPM), which is a good debt to have!

But debt can also be a dangerous foe. Credit card debt is a classic example, with its sky-high interest rates. It's like buying a cup of coffee that costs you a ten-dollar bill. This is bad debt—a burden that weighs you down and hinders your progress. Back to our rental property example: You need a net positive cash flow coming from OPM. If the rental becomes a net negative cash flow situation, it becomes a cash cow draining your financial assets. This investment debt is now bad. Also, having a rental property sit without renters for several months at a time is another example of bad debt. When you are looking at investment debt of any kind, ensure that you will get a net positive cash flow from it or move on to another investment opportunity.

The key, winner, is to discern the difference. Borrow strategically for things that appreciate in value or improve your earning power. But avoid the allure of quick gratification through high-interest debt. It's a trap that keeps you on a treadmill, running in place financially.

The Psychological Toll: How Debt Steals Your Victory

Debt isn't just a financial burden; it's a mental and emotional one as well. Constant worry about payments can be a relentless foe, draining your energy and stealing your peace of mind. Imagine the weight of a heavy shield slowing you down in battle—that's the effect debt has on your spirit.

I know the emotional toll of insurmountable debt very well. The emotional anguish of depression just filled me up and boiled over. Extreme anxiety would overtake me, just looking in the mailbox and seeing the different colored envelopes—some even saying, "Final notice!" I would dodge phone calls because I didn't want to talk to the bullies on the other end. I felt ashamed of my situation and helpless to correct it.

Debt can also strain relationships. Financial stress is a leading cause of arguments between partners, creating tension and division where there should be unity. It can make you feel trapped and powerless, limiting your options and pushing your dreams further out of reach. Understanding this psychological impact is crucial. It can motivate you to manage and eliminate your debt so that you can live a healthier and happier life. It's a wake-up call to action, a reminder that eliminating debt isn't just about numbers—it's about reclaiming your well-being and forging a path to a brighter future.

The True Cost of Debt: Beyond the Numbers

The price tag of debt goes far beyond the initial loan amount. Interest, the hidden enemy, silently adds up over time, turning a small debt into a mountain. Credit card interest rates, for example, can be like a relentless thief, stealing a significant portion of your hard-earned money. But interest isn't the only cost. Processing charges, late fees, and other penalties can further erode your financial strength. These extras are like the dragon's fiery breath, inflicting unexpected damage on your resources.

The long-term impact of debt can be even more devastating. A high debt load can damage your credit score, making it harder and more expensive to borrow money in the future. Imagine needing a car or house loan but being forced to pay a higher interest rate because of past debt. It's a disadvantage that hinders your progress. Debt also limits your ability to save and invest. Every dollar you send towards debt payments is a dollar you can't use to build an emergency fund, invest in your future, or pursue your financial goals. It's like being forced to use your battle gear for everyday tasks, leaving you unprepared when a real challenge arises.

The Call to Action: Knowledge is Power

By understanding the true cost of debt, you gain the power to defeat it. This knowledge is your weapon, the sword that cuts through the dragon's deception. It empowers you to make informed borrowing decisions and prioritize paying off existing debt.

In the next chapter, we'll move from theory to action. We'll explore strategies for assessing your financial situation in detail, creating a clear picture of your income, expenses, and debt. This knowledge will be the foundation for crafting a personalized battle plan to slay the debt dragon and claim your financial freedom. The victory awaits, champion. Are you ready to claim it?

CHAPTER FOUR

KNOWING YOUR BATTLEFIELD:

ASSESS YOUR FINANCIAL LANDSCAPE

E very champion understands the importance of scouting the battlefield before a fight. Here, we'll assess your financial landscape—income, expenses, debt, and credit score. Even though this assessment will probably leave you feeling depressed, it is important to get through it and onto the other side. This intel is crucial for crafting a winning battle plan to slay the debt dragon and claim financial freedom.

Know Your Resources: Income Under the Microscope

You'll need to gather intelligence on your financial resources. Start by identifying all your income streams. This includes your regular salary, any side hustle you may have, investments, rental income, or government benefits. Every dollar coming in is ammunition for the fight ahead. Knowing your total income is essential for creating a budget and determining how much firepower you can use against your debt.

Identifying Your Spending Habits: Expenses—Big and Small

Next, we need to map out the financial terrain. List all your monthly expenses, both fixed and variable. Fixed expenses are like the constant presence of enemy forces on the battlefield—rent, mortgage, utilities, and insurance. Variable expenses are more fluid, like groceries, transportation, and entertainment. Be honest and thorough, leaving no stone unturned. Include every expense, no matter how small. That includes your daily Starbucks java and your monthly pedicure. A penny saved is a penny earned, and every dollar you can free up strengthens your position.

Confronting the Enemy: Taking Stock of Your Debts

Now, it's time to confront the enemy head-on—your debt. Create a detailed inventory of all your debts, including credit cards, student loans, car loans, and other outstanding balances. Record the current balance, interest rate, and minimum monthly payment for each debt. This intel helps you understand the full scale of the enemy force and the resources they're consuming.

Analyzing your income, expenses, and debts can help you gain a clear picture of your current financial situation. This will help you understand the total amount of debt you owe and how much you need to pay each month to stay current. Are you living within your means, or are your expenses outpacing your income? This knowledge is essential for crafting a winning strategy to vanquish your debt and secure financial freedom.

Building Your War Room: Creating a Detailed Debt Inventory

A detailed debt inventory is your war room, a central command center for tracking your enemy. This comprehensive list of all your debts allows you to see the full scope of the challenge and prioritize which debts to tackle first.

You can start by listing each debt with the following details: creditor's name, total balance, interest rate, minimum payment, and due date. This is an expansion of the list made in the prior step. Think of it as gathering intel on each enemy soldier—their strength, weaknesses, and location.

Prioritizing Your Targets: Choosing a Debt Repayment Strategy

There are two main battle plans for debt repayment: the snowball method and the avalanche method. The snowball method prioritizes paying off the smallest debts first. This can lead to quick wins and a boost in morale, keeping you motivated in the fight. Imagine defeating smaller enemy outposts to gain momentum and resources.

The avalanche method, on the other hand, focuses on paying off debts with the highest interest rates first. This saves you more money in the long run by reducing the total interest you pay over time. Think of it as taking out the enemy's heavy artillery first, neutralizing their most dangerous weapons.

There is a third option—the one I consider to be the most beneficial. The one main problem with both methods—snowball or avalanche—is that they are static. What we mean is that they concentrate primarily on one single debt at a time. Some people need this focus and continuity in their battle strategy, and that is totally acceptable. However, a dynamic path that incorporates both strategies together focuses on making the most advantageous monthly payment. This combination method helps you pay off your debts in the least amount of time with the lowest cost. More on this option will be discussed in the next chapter.

Choose the strategy that best suits your temperament and financial situation. Organize your debt list according to your chosen method. Having all your debts in one place, prioritized for attack, makes it easier to craft a targeted repayment plan and track your progress toward victory. Once a debt dragon has been slayed, remember to redirect that payment towards the next debt dragon, and soon.

Maintaining Intelligence: Understanding Your Credit Score

Your credit score is your financial reputation, a number that tells lenders how trustworthy you are—your creditworthiness. It affects your ability to borrow money in the future and the interest rates you'll be offered. A higher credit score signifies a lower-risk borrower earning better loan terms and lower interest rates.

Several factors influence your credit score, with payment history being the most critical. Making on-time payments strengthens your score, while late or missed payments damage it. These damages are cumulative, and it can take up to 7 years before a single late or missed payment can roll off. Vehicle repossessions and house foreclosures are derogatory and can stay on your credit report for up to 7 years. Your payment history is critical, so making regular payments, even the minimums, helps.

I once owned a Saturn SUV. The creditor I had the auto loan through decided one day to sell the loan to another company. I kept on making payments to the original lender because I was not told of the loan transfer for almost three months. During that time, the new lender decided to hit me with late fees and missed payments. They never attempted to collect the payments made to the original lender. Over a short period of time, the fees and penalties piled up, and I started missing regular payments. I didn't have the finances to fight them in a court battle, so I told them to just pick up the vehicle, and they did—they repossessed it a few days later. That decision affected me, my credit report, and my financial position for the next seven years.

Soon after the repossession issue, I started having medical issues that strained my finances. Now, I was missing monthly mortgage payments. After several months of hit-and-miss payments, the mortgage lender issued a foreclosure notice. This battle, however, I was not willing to lose. I had to make several sacrifices and delay gratification. Top ramen noodles, bologna, and off-brand cereal became my go-to meals. I spent all my free time doing yard work, playing video games, and watching movies—absolutely no external entertainment. But after 10 months I was victorious in regaining control of my house and mortgage payments.

Credit utilization, the amount of your available credit you're using, also plays a role. Keeping your credit card balances low improves your score. Your overall utilization should be under 30% but not 0% if you want to keep your credit score higher. Yes, you heard us right—you need to maintain some unsecured credit debt if you're going to max out your score. We highly recommend using the unsecured credit line that has the lowest interest rate. You will also want to keep the revolving balance high enough that you can make the minimum payment on time without zeroing out the balance, while low enough you can pay the balance due off in a single payment if an issue arises.

The length of your credit history matters as well. A more extended history demonstrates a track record of responsible credit management. New credit inquiries and your credit types can also impact your score. Too many inquiries (3 or more) can lower it while having a mix of credit cards and loans can improve it. We also highly recommend having at least one secured credit card in the mix. It helps to add to your overall credit structure, and if something happens, the card is backed by a security deposit.

You can check your credit score through various online services or credit bureaus. Knowing your score is crucial for understanding your financial health and how lenders view you. If your score is lower than desired, you can take steps to raise it over time. You should also check your credit report for collections, liens, and judgments. Not only do these issues damage your credit score, but they may also be there mistakenly, and reporting these types of issues to the credit bureaus can help them disappear and improve your credit score.

You can steadily improve your financial standing by following best practices like paying bills on time, keeping credit card balances low, avoiding unnecessary credit inquiries, and checking your credit report for mistakes.

You've gathered valuable intelligence by assessing your financial situation and understanding your credit score. We'll leverage this intel in the next chapter to craft a winning battle plan. We'll explore setting clear financial goals, developing a realistic budget to optimize your resources, and choosing a debt repayment strategy that aligns with your strengths. These tactics will be your weapons in the fight for financial freedom. So, champion, are you ready to turn the tide and conquer your debt?

Chapter Five

CHARTING YOUR COURSE:

Crafting a Debt Elimination Battle Plan

E very champion needs a plan. Here, we'll forge a strategy to eliminate your debt and claim financial freedom. This battle plan involves setting clear goals, crafting a realistic budget, and choosing the right debt repayment method. These tactics will keep you focused and motivated on your path to victory.

Setting Your Sights: Defining Your Financial Goals

The first step is establishing clear financial goals—your guiding stars on this journey. These goals will keep you laser-focused and provide a target for which to strive. Start by envisioning what you desire to achieve. Do you seek to demolish your credit card debt? Perhaps building a nest egg for a down payment or an emergency fund is your priority.

Make your goals **SMART**: **S**pecific, **M**easurable, **A**chievable, **R**elevant, and **T**ime-Bound. For instance, instead of a vague desire to "pay off debt," set a goal like "I will conquer $5,000 of credit card debt within the next year." This is Specific (amount), Measurable (trackable progress), Achievable (broken down into monthly payments), Relevant (improves financial health), and Time-Bound (one-year deadline).

Write your goals and keep them prominently displayed—on your refrigerator, workspace, or planner. I prefer to write mine on note cards or flashcards and read them daily, along with my affirmations. Regularly seeing your goals constantly reminds you of your purpose and fuels your motivation.

Building Your War Chest: Creating a Realistic Budget

A realistic budget is your financial war chest, the foundation for managing your money and eliminating debt. Similar to assessing your financial situation, list your monthly income and expenses. However, this time, the focus is on streamlining your spending and freeing up resources for debt repayment.

Could you identify areas where you can cut back on expenses? This may involve reducing takeout meals, canceling unused subscriptions, or finding more affordable alternatives. Remember those ramen noodles from before? They and peanut butter became my daily lunch instead of joining my coworkers at restaurants. Reading books instead of going to the movies was another decision I made to cut my expenses. I'm sure there are plenty of minor cuts or changes that you can make in the short term. Every bit adds up. It's not necessarily the large thing that matters but the small, repetitive things that have the most impact.

Be honest with yourself about what's truly essential and what changes you can realistically implement. As with all significant accomplishments in life, making sacrifices is necessary for achieving debt-free living. I had to put a hold on my daily iced tea from Starbucks and stopped going to fast-food joints for the "quick" food fix.

Delaying your gratification not only promotes unnecessary debt accumulation but also provides time to determine if the purchase is actually necessary. I have often found that when I put off purchasing an impulse buy to think more about it, I actually don't need it and usually forget about it. Frivolous spending and impulse shopping are probably two of the reasons how you got into your situation—so stop it! If you are having difficulty overcoming needless spending, try to figure out what is triggering this habit. Once the trigger is identified, you can then devise ways to manage the trigger and prevent the impulse purchase.

Once you've identified areas for reduction, create a new budget reflecting these changes. Allocate a portion of your income toward essential expenses like rent, utilities, and groceries. Then, designate a specific amount for debt payments. Strive to pay more than the minimum amount each month. This speeds up principal reduction and minimizes interest accrued. Even an extra $5 can help in the long run. If there is room in your budget, then target a specific debt that you can make larger payments towards.

You can include a savings category in your budget, even if it's initially a small amount. Building an emergency fund protects you from resorting to debt when unexpected expenses arise. I opened a savings account with a bank I never used, set up a transfer to that savings account directly from my paycheck for $25, and completely "forgot" about it. After a few years, I had accumulated a little over $2,000 in a "sleeper" account. So, I doubled my bi-weekly transfer, and my sleeper account grew twice as fast.

As your financial situation improves, you can gradually increase your savings. Keep in mind that your emergency fund is precisely for that—emergencies! Your "rainy day" money should never be used for anything but emergencies.

Sticking to Your Guns: Maintaining Budget Discipline

Discipline is a warrior's virtue, and it's also crucial here. Adhere to your budget as closely as possible. Track your spending and adjust as needed. This ensures you stay on track and make steady progress towards your debt elimination goals.

Choosing Your Weapon: Snowball vs. Avalanche

Selecting the right debt repayment strategy is key to conquering your debt. Two prominent strategies exist: the snowball method and the avalanche method. Each has its strengths—choose the one that best suits you.

The snowball method—Dave Ramsey's approach to debt elimination—focuses on vanquishing your smallest debts first. List your debts from smallest balance to largest. Make minimum payments on all debts except the smallest one. Focus any extra money on paying off this smallest debt as quickly as possible. Once it's conquered, move on to the next smallest debt, and so on. The snowball method provides quick wins and a sense of accomplishment, keeping you motivated.

The avalanche method prioritizes paying off debts with the highest interest rates first. List your debts in order of highest to lowest interest rate. Make minimum payments on all debts except the highest interest rate. Put extra money towards paying off this high-interest debt as quickly as possible. Once you've conquered it, move on to the next highest-interest debt. The avalanche method saves you more money in the long run by minimizing the total interest you pay.

Both methods are effective, so choose the one that best suits your personality and financial situation. The snowball method might be ideal if you need quick wins for motivation. If saving the most money in interest is your priority, the avalanche method is the better choice.

It is imperative to remember that once a debt dragon has been slayed, any part of your budget you paid that debt with should be added to the next debt dragon to help slay that dragon faster. A portion of that freed-up money can be used to celebrate conservatively. Still, the extra money available should be put towards the next debt elimination in your battle plan.

The snowball and avalanche methods are widely discussed and used to approach debt elimination. However, there is a third strategy, and it can be the most helpful if appropriately executed. The snowball and avalanche methods are static, concentrating primarily on one debt at a time. Some people may need this focus and continuity in their battle strategy, and that is totally acceptable. But a dynamic approach focuses on dealing the most severe blows to your debt each month.

This dynamic method helps you pay off your debts in the least amount of time and at the lowest cost to your wallet. Static approaches typically use lists and spreadsheets to plan and track your debt elimination strategy. But the dynamic approach requires software that reevaluates your specific situation after every financial activity is entered—deposit or debit. This method continually changes to what will cause the greatest result, leading to the fastest and cheapest payoff.

Click on the hyperlink in the resources section of this book to learn more about this software and receive a free simulation based on your current situation.

There is a fourth route as well. We hate to mention it because it is the absolute worst path to take, but it may be the only one available to you. We give great warnings if you use this method. You could go to court and claim bankruptcy. If the judge deems your financial situation desperate, he or she can clean your debt slate. But bankruptcy filing is the most derogatory mark you can have on your credit report.

There are two bankruptcy paths: Chapter 7 and Chapter 13. Chapter 13 bankruptcy is called a "wage earner's plan" because it allows people with regular income to develop a repayment plan for part or all their debt. A debt restructuring, which you commonly hear about with corporations. This type of bankruptcy automatically rolls off your credit report after 7 years. Referred to as "liquidation," Chapter 7 bankruptcy discharges most unsecured debt and will remain on your credit report for 10 years.

With your debt-elimination plan in place, you're ready to act. The next chapter will explore strategies for implementing your plan, including expense reduction, income increase, negotiating with creditors, and maintaining motivation. These tactics will propel you forward on your path to financial freedom. So, champion, are you ready to claim victory over your debt?

CHAPTER SIX

EXECUTING YOUR BATTLE PLAN:

STRATEGIES FOR DEBT ELIMINATION

T he war plan is laid out, champion. Now, it's time to translate strategy into action. Here, we'll explore tactics for implementing your debt elimination plan—reducing expenses, increasing income, negotiating with creditors, and staying motivated. These maneuvers will propel you steadily towards financial freedom.

Double-Edged Sword: Cutting Expenses and Boosting Income

The first strike in your campaign involves a two-pronged attack: minimizing expenses and maximizing income. Reducing expenses frees up resources to tackle your debt. Scrutinize your budget and identify areas where you can tighten your belt. Again, we mention that you will need to make some sacrifices and delay gratification. Are there non-essential expenses you can eliminate or cut back on? Perhaps dining out less, opting for cheaper entertainment, or canceling unused subscriptions are possibilities. Consider cost-saving alternatives—grocery shopping at discount stores or using public transportation. Every dollar saved is a weapon in your arsenal.

Next, explore avenues to increase your income. Take on a part-time job, delve into freelance work, or offer services like tutoring, babysitting, or handyperson skills. Sell unwanted items—clothes, electronics, or furniture—online or at a garage sale. Every extra dollar earned bolsters your debt-fighting capability. This is where a side hustle comes in handy. Several business vehicles, especially in the online arena, require little money and time investment but can provide sizable returns.

Now is a great time to consider turning a hobby (like writing or photography) into an online business (like selling books on Amazon or photo shooting a wedding). You can enter affiliate marketing, establish an agency business, or create an education-based knowledge and coaching platform. The more you cut and the more you earn, the faster your debt crumbles.

Negotiating for Favorable Terms: Engaging with Creditors

Another crucial maneuver is negotiating with your creditors for better terms. Many creditors are open to working with debtors facing repayment challenges. Please contact them, explain your situation honestly and politely, and ask about potential assistance. Chances are, you are not the first person to have financial issues affecting your payments to these creditors, so they have some other solutions that you may not have heard of before. You might be able to secure a lower interest rate, significantly reducing the total interest paid and speeding up debt elimination. Some creditors may even agree to lower minimum payments or offer a temporary pause (forbearance) if you're facing financial hardship.

If you juggle multiple credit card debts, consider a balance transfer to a card with a lower interest rate. Promotional offers exist that allow you to save money on interest and pay off debt faster. Debt consolidation, where you take out a single loan to pay off multiple debts, is another option worth exploring. This simplifies payments and may offer a lower interest rate, but ensure you fully understand the terms and can afford the monthly payments. Negotiating with creditors can be challenging, but it can significantly enhance your debt management and elimination capabilities.

An alternative route is to use any retirement funds you have available. Using a loan from your 401k has many advantages, such as it can be used for debt consolidation, the interest collected goes back into your retirement account, and the interest rate charged is typically at the 12-month average or higher return value of your account. Cashing in a portion of your IRA can also help, although there might be some early withdrawal penalties to consider, so you will want to research this path thoroughly. Please keep in mind that retirement funds are for precisely that—retirement! So, any withdrawals may have some impact on those funds. Research is key.

Staying the Course: Maintaining Motivation Through Setbacks

Staying motivated is the fuel that propels you forward. Debt elimination is a marathon, not a sprint, so maintaining focus and commitment is vital. Here's how you can stay fired up and overcome setbacks:

- **Celebrate Milestones, Big and Small**: Every debt conquered and every milestone reached is a victory. Acknowledge your progress and reward yourself. This reinforces positivity and motivation.

- **Keep Your Goals Visible**: Write down your financial goals and display them prominently—on the fridge, in your planner, or anywhere you'll see them regularly. These constant reminders fuel your determination.

- **Build a Support System**: Share your goals with friends and family and seek their encouragement and support. Consider joining a debt elimination support group or online community. Sharing experiences and learning from others is motivating and helpful.

- **Adapt and Overcome**: Life throws curveballs, and setbacks are inevitable. Don't let an unexpected expense or financial hurdle derail you. Revisit your budget and plan, make necessary adjustments, and keep marching forward. Flexibility is a skill with remarkable outcomes that everyone should learn. Remember, setbacks are part of the journey, and unwavering commitment to your goals will see you through.

By employing these strategies, you can maintain motivation and steadily progress toward becoming debt-free. Remember, baby steps—forward motion, no matter how small—is still forward motion. Progress is the focus, not perfection. I have found that it is the small, repetitive actions and behaviors that make the most impact.

With your debt-elimination plan in action, you're well on your way to financial freedom. The next chapter will explore how to thrive in a debt-free world. We'll discuss building and maintaining an emergency fund, adopting smart spending and saving habits, and investing for your future to build wealth. These steps will solidify your financial health and propel you toward long-term financial success.

CHAPTER SEVEN

THE DEBT-FREE ADVANTAGE:

BUILDING A SECURE FINANCIAL FUTURE

C ongratulations, champion! You've conquered the mountain of debt and reached the summit of financial freedom. But the journey doesn't end here. Maintaining peak financial health requires continued vigilance. This chapter equips you with the tools to build a robust emergency fund, cultivate smart spending habits, and invest strategically for a prosperous future.

Building Your Fortress: The Emergency Fund

Imagine an emergency fund as your financial castle—a secure haven protecting you from life's unexpected storms. This savings account serves as a safety net for unforeseen expenses—medical bills, car repairs, or job loss. Having this buffer prevents you from resorting to debt when the winds of adversity blow.

Set a clear goal for your emergency fund. A typical target is 3-6 months' worth of living expenses. While it may seem daunting, remember that Rome wasn't built in a day. Start small, contribute consistently, and gradually increase your contributions as your financial situation allows. I started my security net by allocating $20 per paycheck to my savings account. Over time, as I had more money available, I raised that amount in steps to $100.

Keep this safety net readily accessible in a separate savings account, but resist the temptation to dip into it because it's for emergencies only. We suggest creating this emergency fund in a bank that is not your normal bank. This helps to keep you from looking at it and removing funds from it. We call this a "sleeper" account—create it, set the allocation, and forget about it until it is needed.

Regular contributions, like adding a stone to your castle wall each day, will eventually build a formidable financial fortress. Along with increasing your contributions, you can add to your account in other ways. Raise increases can be used to help improve your contributions. I typically receive my annual bonuses in a physical check instead of an ACH transaction, so I would deposit them in my emergency fund instead of spending them. You can also use savings bonds. I would purchase savings bonds in the same amount allocated to the savings account for each paycheck.

Sharpening Your Financial Sword: Smart Spending Habits

Living debt-free demands mastery over your spending habits. Developing financial discipline is your trusty sword, protecting you from frivolous and impulsive purchases and keeping you on the path to long-term success.

You can just craft a budget and wield it with discipline. A budget is your financial roadmap, ensuring you live within your means. List all your income and expenses, allocating funds for essentials like housing, food, and transportation. Remember to include savings for both emergencies and future goals! Avoid impulse purchases—they are the enemy of financial progress. Before drawing your financial sword (your wallet), ask yourself: "Is this a need or a want?" Waiting 24 hours can help you discern genuine needs from fleeting desires.

Credit cards can be powerful tools, but wield them with caution. Only use them for what you can afford to repay in full each month. This avoids the crippling burden of interest charges and protects your credit score. If you struggle with credit card overspending, consider the discipline of using cash or a debit card instead. We also suggest having at least one secured credit card, which can be used as your primary purchasing method. Secured credit cards can be built on savings accounts and CDs, which can slowly grow the account with interest received, providing you with more cash reserves.

Be a keen observer and scrutinize everyday expenses for savings opportunities. Look for sales, use coupons, and seek free or low-cost entertainment. Remember, even small savings accumulate over time, bolstering your financial well-being. The small, repetitive acts and behaviors inflict the most significant impact.

Investing for Your Future: Building Your Financial Kingdom

Debt-free living opens the door to investing—planting financial seeds that grow into a prosperous future. Investing allows your money to flourish over time, providing security for you and your loved ones.

Prioritize saving for retirement. If your employer offers a retirement plan like a 401(k), take full advantage of it, especially if they match your contributions. Contribute the maximum you can comfortably afford. Consider opening an Individual Retirement Account (IRA) if a workplace plan is unavailable. A Traditional IRA invests pre-tax dollars from your paycheck, keeping you open to future taxes when withdrawing the funds. The Roth IRA uses after-tax dollars for investing and prevents future taxes when withdrawing funds at or after the allowed retirement age.

The Traditional IRA can lower your taxable income each year, which is important for tax returns. However, the Roth IRA uses after-tax dollars, lowering the amount you will spend on taxes in the future, which will probably continue to increase. Both IRA options usually use a mutual fund or market index to invest the money in, primarily depending on which financial institution you or your employer use. This minimizes where you can select where your investments occur.

A third IRA option exists—the self-directed IRA. A self-directed IRA is a particular account that allows you to select your investment options. This opens the investment market to municipal bonds, tax liens, rental properties, and rural, commercial, and industrial land properties. These additional markets have a much higher return on investment (ROI), but the returns go back into the fund for reinvestment. The funds in a self-directed IRA are only available for retirement.

Explore diverse investment options, such as stocks, bonds, and mutual funds. Investing might seem intimidating, but abundant resources are available to guide you. Consult a financial advisor to craft an investment strategy aligned with your goals and risk tolerance. Remember, diversification is critical. Spreading your investments across various asset classes like stocks, bonds, and real estate protects you from market fluctuations. It is never a good idea to have all your eggs in one basket. We recommend having multiple baskets—both investments and income streams.

Invest in yourself—your most valuable asset. Expand your knowledge through continuing education or gaining new skills. This can enhance your earning potential and unlock exciting career opportunities. Whether you take courses, attend workshops, seminars, and conferences, or pick up new hobbies, investing in yourself is always a wise decision.

The Debt-Free Advantage: A Life of Freedom and Opportunity

With the knowledge and strategies gleaned from this book, you are now empowered to manage your finances effectively, live within your means, and invest strategically for a prosperous future. Debt-free living grants you immense freedom to pursue your dreams unburdened by financial constraints.

The journey continues—stay informed, continuously learn about personal finance, and remain committed to safeguarding your financial well-being. As you move forward, remember the power of setting clear goals and the immense satisfaction of achieving them. Now, let's reflect on the path you've conquered and celebrate the transformative power of living a debt-free life!

CHAPTER EIGHT

CONCLUSION - CHAMPION YOUR FINANCES:

THE DEBT-FREE VICTORY LAP

C ongratulations! You've reached the summit of this guide—a testament to your dedication to conquering your debt. By now, you've grasped the importance of responsible debt management, assessed your financial landscape, crafted a battle plan, and begun executing it. Remember, champion, debt-free living is attainable, and you possess the tools to make it your reality.

Debt can feel like an insurmountable mountain, but with the right approach, we can break it down into manageable steps. Understanding the difference between good debt, used strategically for growth, and bad debt, a suffocating burden, empowers you to make informed financial decisions. Recognizing how debt affects your mindset and life can be a powerful motivator to take control.

A clear understanding of your financial situation is the foundation for any successful campaign. Scrutinize your income, expenses, and debts to gain a panoramic view of your battlefield. Creating a detailed inventory of your debts allows you to see the full enemy force and prioritize your targets. Knowing your credit score and financial reputation equips you to make better borrowing and financial management choices.

Setting SMART financial goals is the cornerstone of your debt elimination plan. These goals provide a clear target, guiding your efforts and keeping you focused on the prize. A realistic budget is your war chest, ensuring you allocate resources effectively and stay on track. Choosing a debt repayment strategy gives you a defined path to follow.

Remember, victory requires a two-pronged attack—minimizing expenses and maximizing income. Every dollar saved or earned strengthens your position. Negotiating with creditors, your adversaries, can lead to more favorable terms, significantly improving your debt-fighting capability. Above all, staying motivated and overcoming setbacks are crucial for staying on course and achieving your goals.

Debt-free living is a fortress built upon several key pillars. An emergency fund serves as your financial moat, protecting you from unexpected expenses and preventing you from falling back into debt's clutches. Developing smart spending and saving habits ensures you live within your means and avoid accumulating new debt. Finally, investing in your future allows your money to flourish, providing long-term financial security.

Now, armed with the knowledge and tools to achieve a debt-free life, remember, the journey is a continuous pursuit of learning. Stay informed, and keep educating yourself about personal finance. The more you know, the better equipped you are to make informed decisions and adapt to changing financial landscapes.

Share your journey with others—a support system strengthens your resolve. Talking to friends and family about your goals and progress fosters accountability. Joining a support group or online community connects you with others on a similar path, offering motivation and valuable insights.

The road to debt-free living is a marathon, not a sprint. It requires ongoing commitment and effort, but the rewards are immeasurable. Financial freedom grants you peace of mind, the ability to pursue your passions, and the power to make choices that improve your life and the lives of those around you. Please just revise your financial goals regularly and adapt them as needed. Life is a dynamic journey, and your financial goals may evolve as well. Staying flexible and adjusting to new circumstances ensures you remain on the path to financial freedom.

Embrace debt-free living—a gateway to a brighter future. Hold fast to the lessons learned, stay committed to your goals, and savor the peace and freedom that comes with financial liberation. Remember, champion, you have the power to achieve great things!

CHAPTER NINE

MAKE A DIFFERENCE WITH YOUR REVIEW

Unlock the Power of Generosity

"True happiness comes from giving, not getting." - Ben Carson

Helping others, expecting nothing in return makes us happier and more successful. So, let's try to make that happen together. Would you help someone you've never met?

They are like you—or like you used to be—struggling with debt and unsure of where to start. Our mission is to make debt elimination accessible to everyone, and we need your help to reach more people.

Most people judge a book by its cover and reviews. So, here's my ask: please leave a review for this book.

Your review costs nothing and takes less than 60 seconds, but it can change someone's life forever. Your review could help ...

... one more person gets out of debt.

... one more family saves money.

... one more person finds hope.

... one more dream comes true.

If you feel good about helping someone, you are my kind of person. Welcome to the club.

Thank you sincerely.

Your biggest fan, Schulz Publishing!

PS - If you believe this book will help someone, please send it their way.

CHAPTER TE

RESOURCES

E mbark on your "DEBT FREE JOURNEY" and become financially liberated to best serve your family!

Meet my buddy Wes Masterson, who can show you how to use an online tool that will help you eliminate debt in the shortest amount of time possible and be personalized to your unique situation. Feel relieved and hopeful as you take control of your financial future!

It's not just about numbers; it's about the stress and limitations it brings into your life. But what if you could rewrite your financial story? With the **Money Max Account,** we help you navigate out of credit cards, student loans, mortgages, and other debts efficiently without upending your current lifestyle. It's time to regain control and enjoy the peace of mind you deserve.

Learn how to eliminate your debt through **Money Max** today!

Click here for Free Debt Consultation!

Debt Elimination and Personal Finance Education.

Chapter Eleven

REFERENCES

Airbnb. (2023). *About us*. Airbnb Newsroom; Airbnb.com https://news.airbnb.com/about-us/

Colestock, S., Jones, J., &Panzer, M. (2023, November 13). *Tips and tricks to get rid of your debt in a year*. USA Today. https://www.usatoday.com/money/blueprint/debt/debt-free-in-a-year/

Collins, J. L. (2016). *The simple path to wealth: Your road map to financial independence and a rich, free life*. JL Collins.

Conversation Ally. (2024, April 5). *Life after debt: 4 steps to take once you're debt-free*. Conversation Ally. https://www.ally.com/stories/debt/debt-free-lifestyle/

Earn In. (2022, December 20). *Road to a debt-free life: 9 effective debt reduction strategies*. EarnIn.com. https://www.earnin.com/blog/road-to-a-debt-free-life-9-effective-debt-reduction-strategies

Finred. (n.d.). *How to avoid - or break - the debt trap cycle*. Finred. https://finred.usalearning.gov/Money/DebtTraps

Fitzgerald, T. (2023, April 11). *Embark on your debt-free journey*. Members 1st Federal Credit Union. https://www.members1st.org/blog/articles/embark-on-your-debt-free-journey/

Gran, B., & Strohm, M. (2021,October 15). *Debt-free in a year? 10 steps and strategies for paying down debt.* Forbes. https://www.forbe s.com/advisor/debt-relief/debt-free-in-a-year-steps-and-strategies/

Holzhauer, B. (2024, April 5). *The case for being completely debt-free and how it can positively impact your mindset.* CNBC.com. https:// www.cnbc.com/select/being-debt-free-and-how-it-impacts-life/

Johnson, H. (n.d.). *8 amazing things that happen when you finally pay down debt.* TheHub.SantanderBank.com. https://thehub.santa nderbank.com/8-amazing-things-happen-finally-pay-debt/

Lee, J., & Pyles, S. (2023, February 9). *How to get out of debt: 7 tips that work.* NerdWallet.com. https://www.nerdwallet.com/article/fi nance/tips-for-paying-off-debt-from-people-who-did-it

Malcolm, M. (2023, May 10). *From $173,000 in debt to debt-free: My 4-year journey to financial freedom.* TakeTinyAction.com . https://taketinyaction.com/debt-free-my-4-year-journey-to-financ ial-freedom/

Manjunath, Mr. R. (2024, May 19). *Debt-free jour-ney: Practical steps to financial freedom.* LinkedIn.com . https://www.linkedin.com/pulse/debt-free-journey-practical-steps -financial-freedom-manjunath-m-r-sg7fc/

Paup, T. (2023, November 15). *Embarking on a debt-free journey: Strategies for paying off loans.* Carlisle Financial Group. https://www.investcarlisle.com/blog/embarking-on-a-debt -free-journey-strategies-for-paying-off-loans

Philadelphia Federal Credit Union. (2024, May 27). *10 strategies for becoming debt-free in 2024.* PFCU.com . https://www.pfcu.com/financial-education/financial-tips/ft/2024 /03/27/ten-strategies-debt-free-2024

Rainer, A. (2024, March 4). *5 people you need on your debt-free j ourney*.FaithFI.com. https://www.faithfi.com/christian-money-solu tions/5-people-you-need-on-your-debt-free-journey-6469

Ramsey, D. (2003). *The total money makeover: A proven plan for financial fitness*. Thomas Nelson.

Ramsey, D. (2024, May 31). *How to get out of debt*.RamseySo lutions.com. https://www.ramseysolutions.com/debt/ways-to-get-o ut-of-debt

Reaves, R. (2019, November 18). *What no one tells you about the debt-free journey*. CityGirlSavings.com. https://citygirlsavings.com/ what-no-one-tells-you-about-the-debt-free-journey/

Robin, V., Dominguez, J. R., and Tilford, M. (2008). *Your money or your life: 9 steps to transforming your relationship with money and achieving financial independence* (2nd ed.). Penguin Books.

Schulz, M. R. (2024). *Creating daily habits: A simple guide to building healthy routines that achieve your goals, build life skills, and improve productivity*. Schulz Publishing.

Sethi, R. (2019). *I will teach you to be rich: No guilt. No excuses. No BS. Just a 6-weekprogram that works*. Workman Publishing.

Shaw, R. (2023, December 4). *4 steps to living debt-free*. Debt.org. https://www.debt.org/advice/debt-free-living/

Take Charge America. (n.d.). *Life after debt: Money moves to make when you become debt-free*. TakeChargeAmerica.org . https://www.takechargeamerica.org/life-after-debt-money-moves -to-make-when-you-become-debt-free/

Val-Oxlade, G. (2009). *Debt-free forever: Take control of your money and your life*. The Experiment.

Williams, D. (2024, May 7). *Debt-free journey: 10 powerful strategies to eliminating debt*. Linkedin.com

. https://www.linkedin.com/pulse/debt-free-journey-10-powerful-s
trategies-eliminating-debt-williams-xnujc/